Peabody Institute Library, Peabody

SO-AZE-295

JUL - - 2004

A0u.

U.S. WARS

THE WAR OF 1812

A MyReportLinks.com Book

Carl R. Green

MyReportLinks.com Books

an imprint of

Enslow Publishers, Inc. E

Box 398, 40 Industrial Road
Berkeley Heights, NJ 07922
USA

MyReportLinks.com Books, an imprint of Enslow Publishers, Inc.

Copyright © 2002 by Enslow Publishers, Inc.

All rights reserved.

No part of this book may be reproduced by any means
without the written permission of the publisher.

Library of Congress Cataloging-in-Publication Data

Green, Carl R.
    The War of 1812 / Carl R. Green.
        p. cm. — (U.S. wars)
    Includes bibliographical references and index.
    Summary: Discusses the major battles, military tactics, and famous
figures of the War of 1812.
    ISBN 0-7660-5092-0
    1. United States—History—War of 1812—Juvenile literature. [1.
United States—History—War of 1812.] I. Title. II. Series.
    E354 .G73 2002
    973.5'2—dc21
                                                    2001008196

Printed in the United States of America

10 9 8 7 6 5 4 3 2 1

To Our Readers:
Through the purchase of this book, you and your library gain access to the Report Links that specifically
back up this book.
The Publisher will provide access to the Report Links that back up this book and will keep these Report
Links up to date on **www.myreportlinks.com** for three years from the book's first publication date.
We have done our best to make sure all Internet addresses in this book were active and appropriate when we
went to press. However, the author and the Publisher have no control over, and assume no liability for, the
material available on those Internet sites or on other Web sites they may link to.
The usage of the MyReportLinks.com Books Web site is subject to the terms and conditions stated on the
Usage Policy Statement on **www.myreportlinks.com**.
In the future, a password may be required to access the Report Links that back up this book. The password
is found on the bottom of page 4 of this book.
Any comments or suggestions can be sent by e-mail to comments@myreportlinks.com or to the address on
the back cover.

Photo Credits: © Corel Corporation, pp. 1 (background), 3; Courtesy of America's Story from
America's Library/Library of Congress, pp. 36, 37; Courtesy of Galafilm: War of 1812, pp. 11, 27;
Courtesy of Hampton Roads Academy, p. 39; Courtesy of James Madison Center/James Madison
University, pp. 13, 30; Courtesy of MyReportLinks.com Books, p. 4; Courtesy of Napoleon: The Man
and the Myth/PBS, p. 41; Courtesy of The Hamilton & Scourge Project, p. 21; Courtesy of the White
House Historical Association, p. 34; Courtesy of Thinkquest Library, p. 24; Department of the
Interior, p. 18; Enslow Publishers, Inc., pp. 23, 35; Library of Congress, pp. 20, 33; National
Archives, p. 17; *Old West Cuts*, © 1995 Dover Publications, Inc., p. 14; Painting by Allyn Cox,
p. 43; Painting by Don Troiani, www.historicalprints.com, p. 1; U.S Senate Collection/by William
Henry Powell, p. 29; U.S. Capitol Collection, p. 19.

Cover Photo: Painting by Don Troiani, www.historicalprints.com

Cover Description: Battle of North Point.

Contents

MyReportLinks.com Books
Great Books, Great Links, Great for Research!

MyReportLinks.com Books present the information you need to learn about your report subject. In addition, they show you where to go on the Internet for more information. The pre-evaluated Report Links that back up this book are kept up to date on **www.myreportlinks.com**. With the purchase of a MyReportLinks.com Books title, you and your library gain access to the Report Links that specifically back up that book. The Report Links save hours of research time and link to dozens—even hundreds—of Web sites, source documents, and photos related to your report topic.

Please see "To Our Readers" on the Copyright page for important information about this book, the MyReportLinks.com Books Web site, and the Report Links that back up this book.

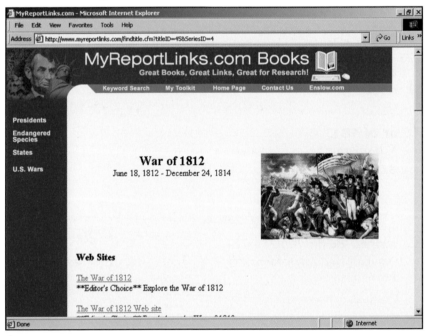

Access:

The Publisher will provide access to the Report Links that back up this book and will try to keep these Report Links up to date on our Web site for three years from the book's first publication date. Please enter **AWE179T** if asked for a password.

Report Links

 The Internet sites described below can be accessed at
http://www.myreportlinks.com

*EDITOR'S CHOICE

▶**The War of 1812**
This site has many brief biographies of British, American,
American Indian, and Canadian individuals involved in the war. It also
has paintings and etchings that depict of a variety of people, maps, and
forts. Links to little known facts and a quiz are also included.

Link to this Internet site from http://www.myreportlinks.com

*EDITOR'S CHOICE

▶**The War of 1812 Web site**
This Web site contains articles, book reviews, pictures, maps, and
sound bites. It also includes many links to other resources, such as
reenactment groups.

Link to this Internet site from http://www.myreportlinks.com

*EDITOR'S CHOICE

▶**The Star-Spangled Banner**
At this Web site you will find a comprehensive history of "The
Star-Spangled Banner." Click on this site to learn about the making
of the flag, its transformations, and more.

Link to this Internet site from http://www.myreportlinks.com

*EDITOR'S CHOICE

▶**The War of 1812**
At this Web site you will find documents relating to the War of 1812,
including An Act Declaring War . . . and the Treaty of Ghent.

Link to this Internet site from http://www.myreportlinks.com

*EDITOR'S CHOICE

▶**An American Hero: Tecumseh**
This site contains Tecumseh's biography, a letter he wrote to William
Henry Harrison, and conflicting accounts of his death in battle.

Link to this Internet site from http://www.myreportlinks.com

*EDITOR'S CHOICE

▶**Winning the Battle of New Orleans**
America's Story from America's Library provides a brief overview of
the Battle of New Orleans. Here you will learn how General Andrew
Jackson led his troops to victory.

Link to this Internet site from http://www.myreportlinks.com

Report Links

The Internet sites described below can be accessed at
http://www.myreportlinks.com

►**War of 1812**
At this Web site you will learn about the causes of the War of 1812, the Chesapeake Affair, the War Hawks, and the outcome of the war.

Link to this Internet site from http://www.myreportlinks.com

►**The American War of 1812**
This site provides newspaper accounts written during the War of 1812. The stories discuss the outcome of battles and campaigns. The site also contains some speeches that Andrew Jackson made to his troops.

Link to this Internet site from http://www.myreportlinks.com

►**The Battle of River Raisin**
This site contains information about the Battle of River Raisin, and includes the names of the officers and privates from Kentucky who fought in it.

Link to this Internet site from http://www.myreportlinks.com

►**Biography of William Henry Harrison**
After winning the Battle of Tippecanoe, William Henry Harrison became an army brigadier general. He also won during the Battle of the Thames, a battle in which his great adversary, Tecumseh, was killed.

Link to this Internet site from http://www.myreportlinks.com

►**Capitol Burning**
After the British set fire to Washington D.C., on August 24, 1814, there was talk that perhaps the seat of government would move to Philadelphia. This site contains all the details of the fire, images of the original Capitol building, and lists important documents that were saved.

Link to this Internet site from http://www.myreportlinks.com

►*Chesapeake*
This site gives information about the USS *Chesapeake*, which was fired upon when its captain refused to allow the British to search it for deserters.

Link to this Internet site from http://www.myreportlinks.com

Report Links

The Internet sites described below can be accessed at
http://www.myreportlinks.com

▶ Constitution
At this PBS Web site you will learn about the legendary USS
Constitution, its colorful history, and the details of its construction
and sailing qualities.

Link to this Internet site from http://www.myreportlinks.com

▶ Dolley Madison on the Burning of Washington
At this Web site you will learn about Dolley Madison's account of the
burning of Washington D.C., including a description of how she saved
a priceless portrait of George Washington.

Link to this Internet site from http://www.myreportlinks.com

▶ Federalist Party
The Federalist Party, mostly comprised of New England shippers, was
opposed to going to war with the British. This site contains a brief
history of the party and its dissolution following the War of 1812.

Link to this Internet site from http://www.myreportlinks.com

▶ General Society of the War of 1812
The General Society of the War of 1812 collects and preserves records,
books, and other documents relating to the War of 1812. This Web site
includes a time line, history, and links to other resources.

Link to this Internet site from http://www.myreportlinks.com

▶ The *Hamilton* and *Scourge* Project
At this Web site you will learn about the American Schooners,
Hamilton and *Scourge*, which capsized on Lake Ontario during
the War of 1812. You will also learn about the war and battles
that were fought.

Link to this Internet site from http://www.myreportlinks.com

▶ James Madison: The Great Little President
At this Web site you will find a comprehensive biography of James
Madison. You will also learn about Madison's foreign policy with
respect to the War of 1812.

Link to this Internet site from http://www.myreportlinks.com

The Internet sites described below can be accessed at
http://www.myreportlinks.com

▶**Napoleon**

By navigating through this PBS Web site you will learn about Napoleon Bonaparte and his involvement in the War of 1812. In particular, you will learn about his ill-fated Russian Campaign of 1812.

Link to this Internet site from http://www.myreportlinks.com

▶**Peace of Ghent**

On December 24, 1814, a peace treaty was signed between the United States and Britain in Ghent, Belgium. This site discusses the negotiations that led to the treaty, and its long term effects.

Link to this Internet site from http://www.myreportlinks.com

▶**Reliving History: the War of 1812**

This is a very informative site that contains photos of reenactments, a time line of history, biographies of key figures, and the causes of the war and its aftermath. There are also maps and a quiz.

Link to this Internet site from http://www.myreportlinks.com

▶**Saving History: Dolley Madison, the White House, and the War of 1812**

The White House Historical Association provides interesting information about Dolley Madison with regard to a letter she wrote during the War of 1812 and the portrait of George Washington she rescued from the White House. *Link to this Internet site from http://www.myreportlinks.com*

▶**A Short Chronology, the War of 1812 in the Northwest**

This searchable database contains a time line of detailed events that transpired in the Northwest durring 1812–13, such as Hull's Campaign and the massacre at Fort Dearborn. You can also search the database for the War of 1812, and find links to images and summaries.

Link to this Internet site from http://www.myreportlinks.com

▶**"Star-Spangled Banner" and the War of 1812**

At this Web site you will learn about how Francis Scott Key was inspired to write the National Anthem of the United States.

Link to this Internet site from http://www.myreportlinks.com

Report Links

 The Internet sites described below can be accessed at
http://www.myreportlinks.com

▶**Statistical Summary: America's Major War**
At this Web site you will find statistical information about the War
of 1812, including casualties and other numbers that put the war
in perspective.

Link to this Internet site from http://www.myreportlinks.com

▶**Tippecanoe Battlefield**
This site contains about the Battle of Tippecanoe, which was fought
between American Indians led by Tecumseh's brother, The Prophet, and
General Harrison's troops. When Tecumseh returned months after the
battle, he made a decision to fight alongside the British.

Link to this Internet site from http://www.myreportlinks.com

▶**War of 1812**
By navigating through this Web site you will find a brief explanation of
the causes of the War of 1812. You will also learn about the British
attack on the capital of the United States.

Link to this Internet site from http://www.myreportlinks.com

▶**War of 1812**
At this Web site you will find a brief overview of the War of 1812.
Here you will learn about the causes, the war itself, and the outcome.

Link to this Internet site from http://www.myreportlinks.com

▶**The War of 1812: Niagara to Stoney Creek**
At this Web site you will find a brief history of the Battle of Stoney
Creek. The site provides descriptions of the battle site, maps, and vivid
images that depict the people and places related to the battle.

Link to this Internet site from http://www.myreportlinks.com

▶**The War of 1812: Second War for Independence**
At this Web site you will find an overview of the War of 1812,
summaries of campaigns, and descriptions of some of the key players.

Link to this Internet site from http://www.myreportlinks.com

War of 1812 Facts

▶ **Combatants:**

The United States of America vs. Great Britain, Canadian militia troops, and American Indian tribal allies.

▶ **Casualties:**

Note: Casualty figures for the War of 1812 vary greatly, depending on the sources consulted. Here are generally accepted battle casualties for the three years of fighting. Historians believe that if deaths caused by sickness, disease, and mistreatment of prisoners of war were included, the casualties for each side would more than double.

Total American casualties: 6,765	Total British casualties: 5,279[1]

▶ **A Brief Time Line**

1807—*June 22:* Chesapeake Affair spotlights issue of "Free trade and sailors' rights."

1811—*Nov. 7:* Battle of Tippecanoe slows Tecumseh's efforts to united American Indian tribes.

1812—*June 18:* United States declares war on Britain.

　　　　Aug. 16: Hull surrenders Detroit without a fight.

　　　　Aug. 20: USS *Constitution* captures HMS *Guerrière.*

1813—*Jan. 23:* River Raisin massacre inflames public opinion.

　　　　March 30: British blockade extends from Long Island to the Mississippi.

　　　　Sep. 10: Perry wins crucial Battle of Lake Erie.

1814—*July 5:* Battle of Chippewa Plain proves fighting qualities of United States troops.

　　　　Aug. 24–25: British invasion force burns Washington, D.C.

　　　　Sep. 11: Battle of Lake Champlain stops British thrust into New York.

　　　　Sep. 13–14: Fort McHenry survives a fierce bombardment.

　　　　Dec. 24: United States and Britain sign the Treaty of Ghent.

1815—*Jan. 8:* Americans hail Battle of New Orleans as a great victory.

Battle of Tippecanoe

The treaty that ended the Revolutionary War in 1783 gave the United States independence from Britain. It did not, however, bring an end to conflict between the two nations. After 1803, as war broke out again in Europe, clashes grew more frequent. At sea, American ships found their routes blocked by French and British men-of-war. Out west,

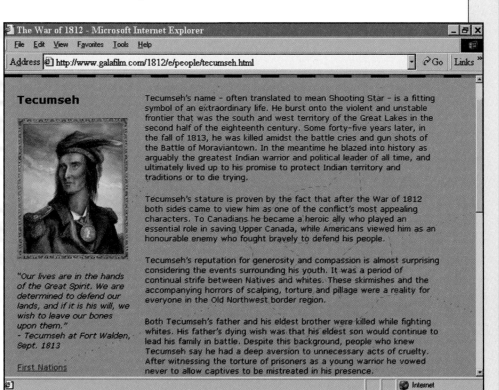

▲ Shawnee Indian Chief Tecumseh led a coalition of American Indian nations in the War of 1812. He is rated as one of the greatest Indian warriors and political leaders of all time.

British officials urged American Indians to fight to keep American settlers out of the Ohio Valley.

The struggle for the huge territory along the Ohio River brought two great leaders face-to-face. William Henry Harrison, governor of the Indiana Territory, managed the settlers' affairs. Tecumseh, son of a Shawnee chief, led the northern Indian tribes. Tecumseh urged the Indians to work together to resist the settlers. He said that all American Indians were "children of the same parents." Therefore, they all owned the land. He felt that unless they all agreed, none of their land should be sold.[1] By 1810, Tecumseh's eloquent speeches had united the Ohio Valley tribes in a strong confederation. His brother, known as The Prophet, added a spiritual message to Tecumseh's call for cooperation among the tribes.

Alarmed by Tecumseh's growing power, the region's settlers turned to Governor Harrison for help. Harrison had fought with General "Mad Anthony" Wayne at the Battle of Fallen Timbers in 1794. Wayne's victory that day opened the way for settlement north of the Ohio River. When he became governor, Harrison signed treaties with the local tribes in which the Indians agreed to open millions of acres of land to the settlers. This alarmed Tecumseh and spurred him to action.

▶ A Stormy Meeting

In August 1810, Tecumseh met with the governor at Vincennes, Harrison's capital in southwest Indiana. The tall Shawnee chief demanded that the treaties be scrapped. "My people once were happy," he said, but now have been "made miserable by the white people, who are . . . always encroaching."[2] Then he returned to his basic belief about

James Madison Center: Image Detail - Microsoft Internet Explorer

File Edit View Favorites Tools Help

Address http://www.jmu.edu/madison/tecumseh/imagewhharrisonbanner.htm   Go Links

▲ *In recognition of his victory at Tippecanoe, President James Madison made William Henry Harrison a brigadier general in command of the Army of the Northwest on March 2, 1813. In October 1813, Harrison's troops won the Battle of the Thames.*

the native's land. "The [recent] sale is bad," Tecumseh said, because "it was made by a part [of the tribes] only."[3]

Harrison argued that the tribes had never been one people. "If such had been [the Great Spirit's] intention," he said, "he would . . . have taught them all to speak one language." The land he had bought, Harrison went on, belonged to the Miami tribe. This meant, he said, that it was none of Tecumseh's business.[4]

Taken aback, Tecumseh called Harrison a liar. As he did so, his warriors drew their tomahawks. Harrison's guards quickly raised their muskets, but the governor told

them to hold their fire. Although the meeting broke up at that point, the two men met again the next day. Tecumseh said he would be a friend—but only if the lands were returned to the American Indians. If not, he vowed, he and his people would fight for the British in the war that was sure to come.

▶ A Hard-Won Victory

Tecumseh increased his efforts to unite the tribes. Urged on by his brother, The Prophet, bands of warriors began raiding frontier settlements. Harrison was forced to ask the federal government in Washington, D.C., for troops. By the fall of 1811, he had recruited nearly a thousand farmers, clerks, and woodsmen. Before risking battle, he put his volunteer militiamen through a tough training program. When the men protested, he offered to let the "weaklings" go home. As he had guessed, no one wanted to be laughed at, and no one left. Once he had their attention, Harrison won the men's hearts by issuing an extra ration of whisky.[5]

In November, Harrison set out to arrest the warriors who had been

The Prophet.

taking part in the raids on the settlements. The trail led to a camp near the Tippecanoe River. Not far away lay the Shawnee village where Tecumseh and The Prophet lived. Tecumseh, however, was not there. He had left to visit some southern tribes. The Prophet, eager for war, told his people that his magic would protect them from bullets. At dawn on November 7, he sent some seven hundred warriors to attack the American camp. Awakened by a warning shot, the soldiers grabbed their muskets and prepared to fight. The warriors charged the camp three times. Each time the American soldiers drove them back. Harrison, ever cool, then sent his horsemen into action. The mounted charge sent the American Indian attackers fleeing into the woods.

The victory was a costly one. The Americans suffered some two hundred casualties, including thirty-seven killed. The Prophet lost at least a hundred men, as well as the trust of his tribe. Tecumseh suffered a harsher blow. When he returned, he found the village in ashes and his confederation in ruins.[6] As he had promised, he trekked north to Canada and signed on to fight for the British.

Harrison's notes on the battle mentioned that British rifles had been found at Prophet's Town. To the settlers, the rifles seemed to prove that the British were arming Tecumseh and his warriors. Like other newspapers, the *Lexington Reporter* ran the report on its front page. "[T]he war . . . is purely BRITISH," its story screamed. "[T]he SCALPING KNIFE and TOMAHAWK of British savages, is now, again devastating our frontiers."[7]

If western settlers had their way, a new war with Britain lay just over the horizon.

"Free Trade and Sailors' Rights"

The Battle of Tippecanoe was only one event in a series of clashes between the United States and Britain. The two nations had been on a collision course ever since the *Chesapeake Affair* of 1807. That incident reminded Americans that winning the Revolutionary War was only a first step toward gaining real freedom. As Benjamin Franklin warned, "The War of Independence is still to be fought."[1]

The *Chesapeake Affair* began with the way Britain's Royal Navy treated its sailors. Pay was poor, voyages were long, and discipline was harsh. Sailors who disobeyed orders were given sixty lashes. Mealtimes brought little relief. The men ate biscuits infested with maggots, and washed down with slimy green water. Given half a chance, sailors often jumped ship. Many of the deserters then went to work for American captains. The pay and food were far better on American ships—and these captains never ordered more than twelve lashes.[2]

The British were involved in a long struggle with Napoleon Bonaparte of France. They believed a strong Royal Navy was necessary to keep French troops from invading their shores. Royal Navy ships therefore needed full crews and their captains constantly searched for deserters.

In June 1807, the British warship HMS *Leopard* sailed on a mission to impress, or seize, deserters who were serving on United States ships. After hailing the USS *Chesapeake*, the captain demanded the right to search the American warship. When the *Chesapeake's* captain refused, the *Leopard* fired three broadsides into the *Chesapeake*. The sudden assault killed three men and wounded eighteen. Caught off guard, the Americans were forced to surrender. A boarding party took four deserters off the ship and the *Chesapeake* limped back to port.[3] The *Leopard*'s captain ignored the fact that some of the men he impressed claimed to be United States citizens.

▶ Tensions Build

British searches of ships were a major grievance. Between 1809 and 1812, British captains did their duty by impressing 750 to 1,000 men a year.[4] However, this was not the only annoyance for Americans.

Britain also wanted to cut off all shipments bound for France. Napoleon struck back by doing all he could to prevent goods from reaching Britain. The resulting blockades and seizures of cargo hurt American shippers. President Thomas Jefferson tried to solve the problem in 1807 by signing the Embargo Act. The act cut off all trade with the rest of the world. No American ships were allowed to leave port. No foreign ships were allowed to dock. The embargo, however, nearly ruined the shipping industry. Jefferson withdrew the act in March 1809, shortly before he left

In 1807, President Thomas Jefferson ▶ signed the Embargo Act, thus cutting off American trade with the outside world. Although he was trying to prevent a problem from escalating, the act did more harm than good.

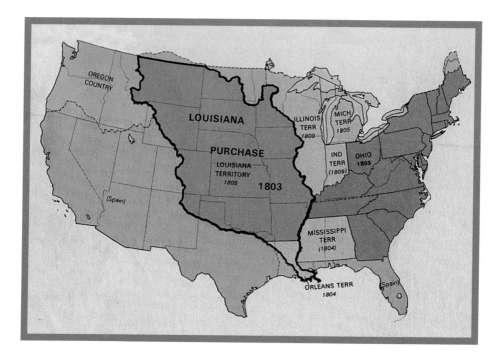

▲ This map shows the territory owned by the United States in 1810.

office. A new act allowed trade to resume—but not with France and Britain.

By this time, Britain had extended its blockade, forbidding trade with any European nation unless the ship carried a British license. Napoleon promptly issued a set of similar orders. In the United States, the cutbacks in trade hurt farmers by driving down crop prices.

In 1810, voters in the South and West handed control of Congress to a group of young men known as the War Hawks. Led by Henry Clay of Kentucky, they ran on a platform that called for "free trade and sailors' rights!" The time had come, Clay said, to defend the "nation's best treasure, honor!"[5]

Not Ready to Fight

Although the War Hawks protested the Royal Navy's hostile actions, shipping was not their main concern. Clay and his supporters focused more on threats to the frontier than on threats to New England farmers. The British, they warned, were arming Tecumseh and his followers. The War Hawks said the only solution was to drive the British out of North America.

The nation, however, was ill prepared for war. On its best day, the army had less than ten thousand men ready for duty. The navy had only sixteen ships under sail. In London, the king's ministers laughed at reports that the United States was about to declare war.

The War Hawks argued that the lack of troops and ships could be fixed. As a first step, they passed a bill that increased the army to thirty-five thousand men. Should war break out, the president was authorized to call up fifty thousand militia troops. A plan to build thirty-two new warships was defeated, however. No one can defeat the Royal Navy, critics said, so why waste money?

Even Jefferson, who had tried to keep the peace, changed his mind. "Every hope . . . is exhausted," he said, "and war or abject submission are the only alternatives left to us."[6] The nation's Second War of Independence was about to begin.

Congressman Henry Clay,
leader of the War Hawks.

"Mr. Madison's War"

On June 1, 1812, President James Madison asked Congress to declare war on Britain. He listed grievances against the British that included seizing sailors and arming American Indians. With the New England states strongly opposed, the House passed the declaration, 79 to 49. The vote was even closer in the Senate. The measure squeaked through the upper house by a vote of 19 to 13. Madison signed the document that committed the nation and its eighteen states to war on June 18. It was the closest vote on any declaration of war in U.S. history.[1]

Madison did not know that Britain had ended its harsh trade restrictions two days earlier. By the time that news reached North America, "Mr. Madison's War" had already begun.

Each side had reasons to feel optimistic. The British Army was stretched thin along the Canadian border, but the Royal Navy ruled the seas. Until more troops could be spared from Europe, the Royal Navy would blockade the Atlantic Coast states. On the American side, Madison knew his navy was outgunned. The solution, his advisers told him, was to launch a land invasion of Canada.

◀ *President James Madison.*

▶ A Three-Pronged Disaster

On paper, the American Army had thirty-five thousand soldiers. In reality, Madison could call on only 11,700 regulars. Of these, five thousand were recruits who were still learning the arts of war. As a result, the thrusts into Canada were made with mixed forces of regular troops and militia volunteers. Some of the officers who led these troops were among the nation's best. Others, as events proved, were hopelessly inept.

Hoping for a quick victory, the War Department approved a three-pronged assault along the Great Lakes.

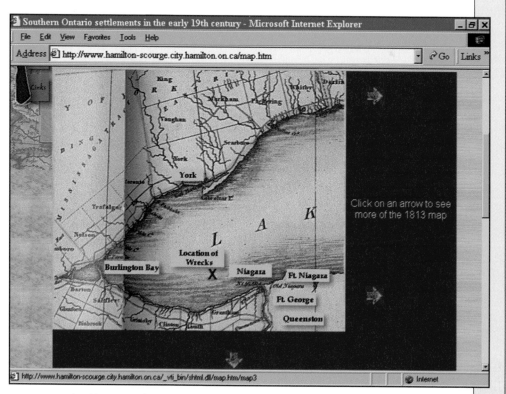

▲ This map shows the locations of the battles at Burlington Bay, Fort George, Fort Niagara, and Queenston.

All three attacks failed. The worst setback took place at Detroit. General William Hull opened the campaign by crossing the Detroit River and seizing the Canadian town of Sandwich. If the elderly general had acted swiftly, he could have moved on to win control of the region by capturing Fort Malden. Instead, alarmed by rumors that his men were outnumbered, he retreated to Detroit. When the British laid siege to the town, Hull lost his nerve. Rather than risk further bloodshed, he surrendered on August 16 without a fight.

General Stephen Van Rensselaer's October campaign at Niagara, on the border of Canada and New York, ended just as badly. With his men eager for a fight, he launched an attack across the Niagara River. The first boat reached the far shore, but the other boats failed to follow. Someone, it turned out, had loaded all the oars into the first boat. Three days later, the Americans crossed in force and drove the British defenders toward Queenston. When the forward units called for reinforcements, the militia troops refused to cross the river. The sight of dead and wounded men had robbed them of their will to fight. They watched from a safe distance as the British cut their friends to ribbons.[2]

Henry Dearborn's campaign along Lake Champlain met a similar fate. On November 19, his soldiers crossed the river at Plattsburgh and captured a blockhouse. In the darkness, the poorly trained troops became confused and opened fire on each other. After that mishap, they carried their wounded back across the river. There they found that Dearborn's militia units had refused to cross into Canada. Crossing the border, many volunteers believed, would lead to their becoming part of the regular army. Dearborn gave up and sent the army into winter quarters.[3]

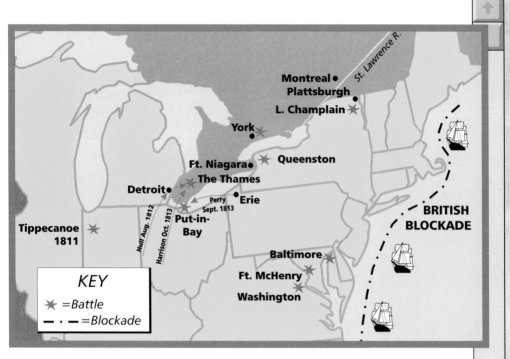

▲ *This map shows the major northern campaigns of the War of 1812.*

▶ A Different Story at Sea

At a time when the war seemed lost, American morale received a big boost. In battle after battle, United States warships gave the Royal Navy a sound thumping. The victories surprised both sides, because the U.S. Navy was dwarfed by the British fleet. As one writer put it, Britain had more warships than the United States fleet had guns.[4]

Captain Isaac Hull, nephew of General William Hull, took the lead in showing what American ships could do. His epic battle took place a few days before news of his uncle's defeat at Detroit reached the East Coast. Hull was sailing off New England in the USS *Constitution* when he met the HMS *Guerrière* on August 19. As he came within fifty yards of the enemy, Hull shouted, "Now boys, pour

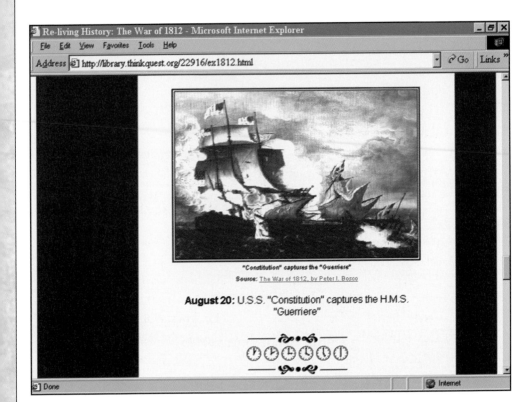

Re-living History: The War of 1812 - Microsoft Internet Explorer

File Edit View Favorites Tools Help

Address http://library.thinkquest.org/22916/ex1812.html   Go   Links

"Constitution" captures the "Guerriere"

Source: The War of 1812, by Peter I. Bosco

August 20: U.S.S. "Constitution" captures the H.M.S. "Guerriere"

Done   Internet

▲ The USS Constitution *became known as "Old Ironsides" because the British saw their cannon balls bounce off the "iron sides" of the ship. The* Constitution *defeated the HMS* Guerrière *on August 20, 1812.*

it into them."[5] With all the guns on each side of the ship firing in turn, Hull's gunners loosed a series of broadsides that smashed the British frigate's masts and rigging. The British fought back, only to see their cannon balls bounce off the *Constitution*'s heavy timbers. "Huzzah!" someone shouted. "Her sides are made of iron."[6] By this time, the *Guerrière* was so badly damaged that her captain lowered his flag as a signal that he was ready to surrender. The *Constitution* sailed on into history with the proud nickname "Old Ironsides."

American warships ruled the seas during the fall of 1812. The USS *United States,* under Captain Stephen Decatur, nearly blasted HMS *Macedonian* out of the water. The sloop (a small warship) USS *Wasp* won a firefight with HMS *Frolic.* Its sister ship, the USS *Hornet,* defeated HMS *Peacock.* Adding to British woes, privately owned American ships called privateers were seizing the king's merchant ships. In six months, this "cheapest and best Navy" captured 450 vessels, or "prizes" of war. The USS *Rossie,* with Joshua Barney at the helm, took eighteen prizes valued at $1.5 million.[7] To round out the year, the *Constitution* returned to action by smashing HMS *Java.*

On December 10, Washington, D.C., honored its naval heroes with a grand ball. The guests cheered at the sight of British battle flags hanging on the walls of the ballroom. It was a gala affair, but the good times were already ending. The string of losses had alarmed the British government. Their admirals revised the Royal Navy's battle plans and sent more ships to North America. Seven were men-o-war, the battleships of their day. To combat this fleet of nearly a hundred ships, the U.S. Navy had less than twenty ships under sail. By 1813, the blockade of eastern United States ports and harbors had begun in earnest.

"Don't Give Up the Ship!"

The tide of the sea war shifted in the spring of 1813. The U.S. Navy was still fearless, but courage was not enough. The Royal Navy tightened a blockade that stretched from Long Island to the Mississippi. American warships lay idle, bottled up in their home ports.

In June, HMS *Shannon* and the USS *Chesapeake* met off the New England coast. This time the British gunners held the upper hand. The first exchange badly damaged the *Chesapeake* and wounded Captain James Lawrence. As his men carried the dying hero below, he gave his final order: "Don't give up the ship!"[1] The brave words would later become a naval legend, but firepower won this battle. After a gory free-for-all in which both captains died, the crippled *Chesapeake* surrendered.

▶ The Blockade Hits American Pockets

Even before the war started, trade restrictions had hurt American exports. After 1812, the British blockade cut even deeper. The damage can be seen in the decline in trade. In 1807, Americans shipped goods worth $130 million to foreign markets. That number fell year by year, dropping to a low of $7 million in 1814. The government's main source of income declined at the same time. Import duties fed $13 million into the U.S. Treasury in 1811. Three years later, customs collectors took in less than half that amount.[2]

The British fine-tuned the blockade to play one section of the country against another. To encourage New

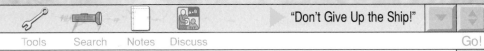

The War of 1812: Forts - Microsoft Internet Explorer

File Edit View Favorites Tools Help

Address http://www.galafilm.com/1812/e/catalogues/peop_cockburn.html   Go   Links

http://www.galafilm.com/1812/e/people/cockburn.html   Internet

▲ *George Cockburn was a ruthless British admiral who looted and burned American towns because his ships needed fresh supplies.*

England's peace movement, all ports north of New London, Connecticut, were left open. Local farmers earned good profits by selling food products in Canada. The British policy changed when the war in Europe ended. In May 1814, the Royal Navy extended its blockade to all United States ports and harbors. President Madison struck back with a trade embargo. The act reduced the flow of supplies to Canada, but did its greatest harm at home. Prices rose and incomes fell as trade came to a standstill.

To make matters worse, British warships sailed into American bays and sent raiding parties ashore. The people

of Lewes, Virginia, fought off a raid in April 1813. The Virginia towns of Fredericktown and Georgetown were not as lucky. Admiral George Cockburn's men looted and burned those unfortunate Maryland towns. Cockburn ordered the raids because his ships needed fresh food. If the sight of burning houses brought the horrors of war home to the American people, so much the better, he thought.[3]

▶ A Border War Turns Nasty

On the Canadian border, the year 1813 began with a massacre. The action started when General James Winchester captured a British outpost on the River Raisin. Even though he was on enemy soil, Winchester failed to post guards. General Henry Procter's troops, backed by Indians, launched a surprise attack at dawn. Winchester surrendered after a brief battle in which many of his Kentuckians were scalped. As he led his men away, Procter left some thirty wounded Americans behind. On January 23, a band of Indians found the helpless men and killed them.[4] "Remember the River Raisin" soon became an army rallying cry.

In April, U.S. Navy ships sailed across Lake Ontario with a force of sixteen hundred troops. Led by the explorer Zebulon Pike, the invaders quickly seized York, the capital of upper Canada. As the Americans searched the town, a powder storehouse blew up. Pike died in the blast, along with a number of his men. The survivors looted some homes and burned government buildings. Seven months later, British troops invaded New York and evened the score. After capturing Fort Niagara, General Gordon Drummond burned Buffalo, Lewiston, and Black Rock.

▶ Two Great Victories

American forces won two key battles that year. The first victory added Oliver Hazard Perry's name to the history books. The young naval officer set out for Lake Erie in March with orders to support the army's invasion of Canada. When he arrived, Perry found only two small ships waiting for him. He put his crews to work felling trees and building four new ships. Pittsburgh's ironworks provided anchors, stoves, and cannon balls. Ox teams pulled five more ships up the Niagara River to the lake. By August, Perry was ready to tackle the British fleet.

▲ An artist's rendition of the Battle of Lake Erie.

James Madison Center: Image Detail - Microsoft Internet Explorer

File　Edit　View　Favorites　Tools　Help

Address http://www.jmu.edu/madison/tecumseh/imagebattlethames.htm Go Links

Done　Internet

Tecumseh, the great warrior chief, died at the Battle of the Thames on October 18, 1813.

On paper, Perry was stronger, nine ships to six. The British ships, however, had thirty-five long guns to Perry's fifteen.[5] When the two fleets met on September 10, Captain Robert Barclay's long guns peppered the American ships. Perry ordered his ships to move in and fire from close range. Midway through the battle, he was forced to leave his sinking flagship. Moving to the *Niagara*, he raked the British ships with deadly broadsides. By three o'clock in the afternoon the battle was over. Perry pulled out a scrap of paper and scribbled a message to General William Henry Harrison. "We have met the enemy, and they are ours," he wrote to the victor of Tippecanoe. "Two ships, two brigs, one schooner and a sloop."[6]

Harrison next mapped out a plan to give the hated General Procter a sound beating. The frontier campaign began when Perry's ships landed Harrison's army on a beach south of Detroit. Fearing he was outnumbered, Procter burned his extra stores and withdrew. Harrison's old foe, Tecumseh, protested but Procter ignored him. On October 4, Procter made his stand between a swamp and the Thames River.

Harrison opened the Battle of the Thames with a two-pronged attack. On one side, mounted riflemen crashed through the woods and broke the British line. On the other flank, his Kentuckians charged through heavy fire to grapple with Tecumseh's warriors. The great chief died in the fierce hand-to-hand fighting that ended in a United States victory.

As the year drew to a close, the news from the Northwest was mixed. The U.S. Navy controlled Lake Erie. The Stars and Stripes again flew over Detroit. As the news spread of Tecumseh's death, many American Indian warriors broke their ties to the British. An American attempt to capture Montreal, however, was beaten back. Both sides were forced to rethink their plans for winning the war.

Chapter 5

"Oh, Say Can You See?"

Britain greeted 1814 with a surge of confidence. Victory over France had freed the army and navy to focus on North America. As a result, British officials thought the United States would give up and beg for peace. That would allow for Britain to reclaim land lost in the Revolution. The British believed that New England, where antiwar feeling was strong, might welcome a chance to rejoin the Empire.

British generals mapped out a complex plan of attack. The first thrust was aimed at what is now the state of Maine. The second looked south to Lake Champlain and the Hudson Valley. If that campaign was successful, New England would be cut off from the Union. While the army did its job, the Royal Navy would attack Washington, D.C., and Baltimore. If successful, the raids would keep the Americans from sending troops to fight the British march south. The final blow was aimed at New Orleans. Whoever controlled that key city could control traffic on the Mississippi River. Victories on all these fronts, the generals promised, would end the war.[1]

▶ Crucial Battles in the North

The campaign to seize eastern Maine went like clockwork. By summer, the British controlled a hundred miles of Maine's coastline. The Lake Champlain campaign did not go as smoothly. On Chippewa Plain, near Niagara Falls, the "Yankee Doodles" (the British name for the American soldiers) proved they could stand up against the British veterans. In the first stage of the battle, both sides ordered

▲ British troops set fire to the White House and most of Washington, D.C., on August 24, 1814. This cartoon shows President James Madison and Secretary of War John Armstrong fleeing from Washington with bundles of papers in their hands.

an attack. Step by step, the two lines advanced, stopping only to reload. The line of British Redcoats crumbled first. When the smoke cleared, five hundred Redcoats and three hundred United States soldiers lay dead or wounded. The Americans had beaten the British Army at its own game.[2]

Two months later, Sir George Prevost kicked off a major British push southward. Prevost should have held a winning hand. Veterans fresh from the European wars formed the backbone of his army of eleven thousand men. Ahead lay Plattsburgh, the key American stronghold on Lake Champlain. The fort was held by only thirty-three hundred troops, backed up by four small warships. However, Prevost made a mistake in judgment and ordered his four-ship navy to attack the United States fleet in

Plattsburgh Bay. Out on the lake, the British long guns held the upper hand. When they sailed into the narrow bay, however, American short-range guns chopped them to bits. Their victory meant the Americans would be able to cut Prevost's supply lines if he marched south. He weighed the odds—and led his army back to Canada.[3]

▶ Washington Burns, Baltimore Triumphs

On August 24, word reached Washington, D.C., that British troops were advancing on the city. President Madison climbed on a horse and rode out to join his army at nearby Bladensburg. At one point, he almost led his

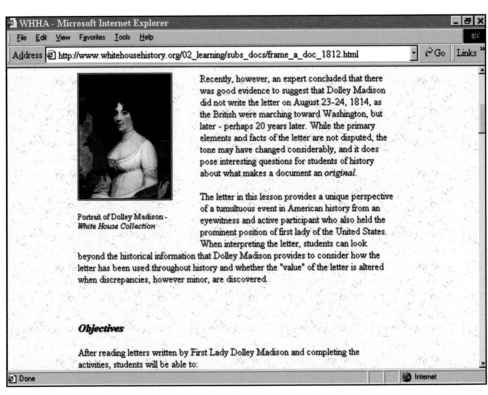

Dolley Madison is remembered for saving a painting of George Washington from the White House.

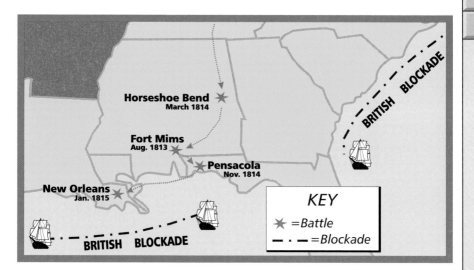

▲ *These were the major battles that took place in the southern United States during the War of 1812.*

party directly into the enemy lines. His presence did little to aid the nervous defenders. The oncoming Redcoats charged the American lines, backed by a barrage of rockets. Frightened by the "comets" swooshing overhead, the militia troops fled. Only a handful of men stayed to fight, led by Joshua Barney and his sailors. Their brave stand ended with Barney leading a suicidal bayonet charge.

Dolley Madison, wife of the president, was one of the few heroes of the day. As friends urged her to flee, she stayed in the White House long enough to load a wagon with valuables. One of the paintings she saved was Gilbert Stuart's fine portrait of George Washington. As she left Washington, the British surged into a nearly empty city. When they entered the White House, they found the table set for dinner. After eating their fill, they set fire to the house, along with much of Washington.[4] As the city burned, a fierce rainstorm swept in and put out many of the fires. In the midst of the storm, the British heard rumors of an approaching army. Their mission over, they returned to their ships to enjoy the victory.

A few weeks later, a similar attack on Baltimore met more resistance. The battle plan called for the Royal Navy to prepare the way by silencing the city's forts. Unlike Washington, Baltimore was well prepared. Fort McHenry and the other forts survived a twenty-five-hour bombardment that began on September 13. Admiral Alexander Cochrane finally admitted defeat and called off the assault. He then set sail for the Gulf Coast.

A lawyer named Francis Scott Key had boarded Cochrane's flagship to arrange the release of a local doctor.

Andrew Jackson led the American troops in the Battle of New Orleans.

Tools   Search   Notes   Discuss   Go!

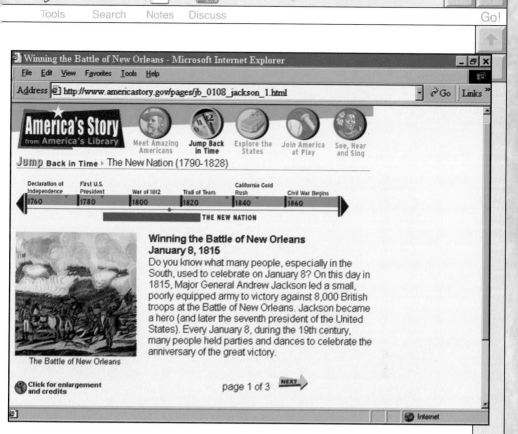

Winning the Battle of New Orleans - Microsoft Internet Explorer

File Edit View Favorites Tools Help

Address http://www.americastory.gov/pages/jb_0108_jackson_1.html   Go Links

America's Story
from America's Library

Meet Amazing Americans   Jump Back in Time   Explore the States   Join America at Play   See, Hear and Sing

Jump Back in Time ▸ The New Nation (1790-1828)

Declaration of Independence   First U.S. President   War of 1812   Trail of Tears   California Gold Rush   Civil War Begins

1760   1780   1800   1820   1840   1860

THE NEW NATION

Winning the Battle of New Orleans
January 8, 1815

Do you know what many people, especially in the South, used to celebrate on January 8? On this day in 1815, Major General Andrew Jackson led a small, poorly equipped army to victory against 8,000 British troops at the Battle of New Orleans. Jackson became a hero (and later the seventh president of the United States). Every January 8, during the 19th century, many people held parties and dances to celebrate the anniversary of the great victory.

The Battle of New Orleans

Click for enlargement and credits   page 1 of 3   NEXT

▲ Two weeks before the Battle of New Orleans, Britain and the United States signed the Treaty of Ghent, which ended the war of 1812.

When the battle started, Key watched from a front-row seat. In the morning, the sight of the American flag still flying above Fort McHenry inspired him to write "The Star-Spangled Banner." The song was an instant hit, but did not become the national anthem until 1931.[5]

The Battle of New Orleans

Andrew Jackson became an American hero in the Battle of New Orleans. Jackson had made a name for himself in a series of bloody battles against the Creek Indians. The Creeks and their British advisers on the western frontier,

had overrun Fort Mims, killing 500 settlers. When he heard rumors of a British attack on New Orleans, Jackson hurried there to take charge.

Recruits flocked to Jackson's side. Jean Laffite and his pirate band were among the volunteers who stepped forward. To even the odds for his handful of troops, Jackson built a line of ramparts (protective barriers) on swampy land south of the city. On January 8, 1815, the British threw their best troops at him in an all-out assault. Thirty minutes later, the Redcoats fell back as volleys of rifle fire cut them down by the hundreds. When they limped away, the British had lost some two thousand men. Jackson had only lost seventy.[6] The victory saved New Orleans—and launched Jackson on the road to the White House.

Americans cheered the Battle of New Orleans as a great military feat. They had no way of knowing that the two nations had signed a peace treaty two weeks earlier. The news, carried by sailing ship, did not reach North America until February 8.

The War Nobody Won

The treaty that ended the War of 1812 was signed in Ghent, Belgium, on December 24, 1814. For the British people, the war with the United States had never been a major concern. Unlike their government, few had any dreams of regaining their lost American colonies. After winning the long struggle with France, they wanted to

Peace of Ghent - Microsoft Internet Explorer

File   Edit   View   Favorites   Tools   Help

Address http://www.hra.org/~06hposth/date.html   Go   Links

What happened on December 24, 1814?

Since August of 1814, five American diplomats tried to negotiate peace with the British in the city of Ghent, in Belgium. On December 24, 1814, the Peace of Ghent was signed to conclude the War of 1812. After several months, the treaty finally fell through. With this document that was signed by delegates from England and the United States, it made sure that no territory changed hands and it restored peace without any promises. As one witty historian put it, "It surrendered nothing except the right to shoot Englishmen," and that was a right no one any longer wished to exercise. The United States had not achieved it's goal in the War of 1812.

With the Treaty of Ghent, both countries agreed to do their best to abolish slavery and it was provided that commissions would be set up to determine the boundary from the St. Croix River west to Lake of the Woods. Also, both countries agreed to use their best endeavors to abolish slavery.

Internet

▲ The Treaty of Ghent officially ended the War of 1812.

enjoy the fruits of peace. For Americans, the Battle of New Orleans seemed to make up for all the earlier defeats. The young nation knew that it had survived a test of its will, as well as a test of its fighting skills.

The peace talks had been dragging on since August. From day one, the British refused to debate the issue of sailors' rights. Both sides then moved to other demands. The American delegates argued that Britain should sign over a big chunk of Canada. That demand was quickly rejected as well. In an effort to protect their American Indian allies, the British proposed that no further settlement should be allowed in the tribal lands in the Northwest. The Americans knew that settlers already were pouring into the territory, so they vetoed that proposal.

In the end, the Treaty of Ghent simply turned the clock back to June 1812. With no clear winner to make demands, no one gained or lost any territory. This was, in truth, "The War Nobody Won."[1]

▶ The War Winds Down Slowly

Captains who set out to sea in December and January did not know the war was over. In February, the USS *Constitution* captured two British sloops-of-war in a forty-minute battle. The USS *Peacock* fired the final broadside of the war on June 30. As the British captain had already told the *Peacock* that the war was over, this was hardly an act of courage. The British proved they could behave just as badly. The government did not release the last of six thousand American prisoners until July.[2]

On the issue of shipping and searches by the British, better times lay ahead. The turning point came that same year, after Napoleon escaped from exile and raised a new army. He challenged the British and met his final defeat

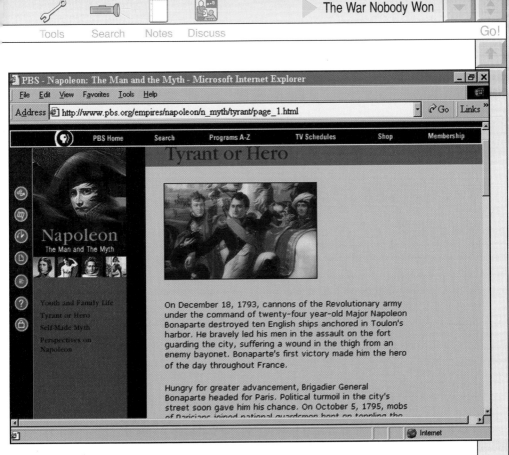

Tools   Search   Notes   Discuss   Go!

PBS - Napoleon: The Man and the Myth - Microsoft Internet Explorer

File   Edit   View   Favorites   Tools   Help

Address http://www.pbs.org/empires/napoleon/n_myth/tyrant/page_1.html   Go   Links

PBS Home   Search   Programs A-Z   TV Schedules   Shop   Membership

Tyrant or Hero

Napoleon
The Man and The Myth

Youth and Family Life
Tyrant or Hero
Self-Made Myth
Perspectives on
Napoleon

On December 18, 1793, cannons of the Revolutionary army under the command of twenty-four year-old Major Napoleon Bonaparte destroyed ten English ships anchored in Toulon's harbor. He bravely led his men in the assault on the fort guarding the city, suffering a wound in the thigh from an enemy bayonet. Bonaparte's first victory made him the hero of the day throughout France.

Hungry for greater advancement, Brigadier General Bonaparte headed for Paris. Political turmoil in the city's street soon gave him his chance. On October 5, 1795, mobs of Parisians joined national guardsmen bent on toppling the

Internet

▲ Napoleon lost his last battle at Waterloo in June 1815.

at Waterloo in June 1815. From that time on, Britain seemed content to live by the rules of "free trade and sailors' rights."

In Canada, the war built a new sense of unity. British and French settlers had fought together during the war. In their eyes, American attempts to invade Canada had been a threat to their life and liberty. When the fighting ended with their borders intact, Canadians felt a surge of pride in themselves and their country.[3]

Effects on the United States

In 1815, the American Congress needed money to pay the nation's bills. One estimate puts the cost of fighting

the war at $158 million, a huge amount for that time.[4] Along the coast and on the northern frontier, people rolled up their sleeves and set to work. There were towns to rebuild and farms to bring back to life.

The government also tackled the problem of national defense. Congress quickly voted to build twenty-one new warships for the navy. Another $8.5 million went to build new forts along the coast. The peacetime army was set at ten thousand men, three times more than before the war. Even this increase sparked a lively debate. Despite the poor performance of some militia units, Americans preferred a volunteer army. They feared that a would-be tyrant might use a strong regular army to overthrow the government.

With the blockade ended, fishermen and whalers put to sea again. Warehouses emptied as shiploads of cotton, rice, and tobacco flowed to foreign markets. New England,

▲ War of 1812 military hero Andrew Jackson later became the seventh president of the United States.

largely untouched by the war, became an industrial center. A combination of new machines, skilled workers, and canny traders created an economic boom. More and more Americans produced their own cloth, tools, and household goods.

Peace brought other changes as well. The New England states met in Hartford, Connecticut, late in 1814 to discuss their grievances with the federal system. Some hotheads wanted to leave the Union, but calmer voices won the debate. When the war ended a few weeks later, the threat was forgotten.

In the South, Andrew Jackson's expedition into Spanish West Florida in 1813 drew little notice. His attack on Pensacola, however, began the process that later would add Florida to the Union.

A Final Word

The United States grew and prospered as the years slipped past. In 1829, a new tariff policy led to a hot dispute with Britain. In London, two members of Parliament talked about going to war over the issue.

"We had better yield a point or two than go to war with the Americans," one said. "Yes," his friend replied. "We shall get nothing but hard knocks there."[5]

The United States still had plenty of growing pains to come. Never again, though, would Britain challenge its freedom and independence.

Highlights

1. "British Losses and American Losses," *The United States at War! War of 1812*, n.d., <http://www.geocities.com /Pentagon/Camp/7624/Warof1812.htm> (August 30, 2001).

Chapter 1. Battle of Tippecanoe

1. Devin Bent, "An American Hero: Tecumseh, a Brief Biography," *James Madison, His Legacy*, n.d., <http://www .jmu.edu/Madison/tecumseh/tecumsehbio.htm> (August 15, 2001).

2. "Tecumseh to Governor Harrison at Vincennes, August 12, 1810," *James Madison, His Legacy*, n.d., <http://www.jmu.edu/Madison/tecumseh/letterharrison. htm> (August 15, 2001).

3. Ibid.

4. Benson J. Lossing, *The War of 1812: A Facsimile of the 1860 Edition* (Somersworth, N.H.: New Hampshire Publishing Company, 1976), p. 192.

5. R. Ernest Dupuy and Trevor N. Dupuy, *Brave Men and Great Captains* (New York: Harper & Brothers, Publishers, 1959), p. 71.

6. Ibid., p. 72.

7. Donald R. Hickey, *The War of 1812: A Forgotten Conflict* (Urbana: University of Illinois Press, 1989), p. 26.

Chapter 2. "Free Trade and Sailors' Rights"

1. Albert Marrin, *1812: The War Nobody Won* (New York: Atheneum, 1985), p. 12.

2. Ibid., pp. 8–10.

3. Donald R. Hickey, *The War of 1812: A Forgotten Conflict* (Urbana: University of Illinois Press, 1989), p. 17.

4. Harry L. Coles, *The War of 1812* (Chicago: University of Chicago Press, 1965), p. 24.

5. Reginald Horsman, *The War of 1812* (New York: Alfred A. Knopf, 1969), p. 18.

6. Coles, p. 35.

Chapter 3. "Mr. Madison's War"

1. Donald R. Hickey, *The War of 1812: A Forgotten Conflict* (Urbana: University of Illinois Press, 1989), p. 46.

2. Margaret L. Coit, ed., *The Life History of the United States: The Growing Years, Vol. 3: 1789–1829* (New York: Time, Inc., 1963), p. 102.

3. Harry L. Coles, *The War of 1812* (Chicago: University of Chicago Press, 1965), p. 69.

4. John Dos Passos, *The Shackles of Power: Three Jeffersonian Decades* (Garden City, N.Y.: Doubleday & Company, 1966), p. 210.

5. Coles, p. 80.

6. "USS Constitution: History Timeline," *Old Ironsides History Page,* n.d., <http://www.ussconstitution.navy.mil/Shiphistoryx.htm> (August 20, 2001).

7. Hickey, pp. 96–97.

Chapter 4. "Don't Give Up the Ship!"

1. Reginald Horsman, *The War of 1812* (New York: Alfred A. Knopf, 1969), p. 73.

2. Harry L. Coles, *The War of 1812* (Chicago: University of Chicago Press, 1965), p. 89.

3. Ibid., p. 93.

4. Horsman, p. 85.

5. Coles, p. 126.

6. Richard Dillon, *We Have Met the Enemy: Oliver Hazard Perry, Wilderness Commodore* (New York: McGraw-Hill Book Company, 1978), p. 153.

Chapter 5. "Oh, Say Can You See?"

1. "Campaigns of 1812–13," *War of 1812,* n.d. <http://www.gatewayno.com/History/War1812.html> (July 30, 2001).

2. Alan Lloyd, *The Scorching of Washington: The War of 1812* (D.C.: Robert B. Luce Co., 1974), pp. 146–147.

3. Ibid., pp. 180–183.

4. David Colbert, ed., *Eyewitness to America: 500 Years of America in the Words of Those Who Saw It Happen* (New York: Pantheon Books, 1997), p. 118.

5. Donald R. Hickey, *The War of 1812: A Forgotten Conflict* (Urbana: University of Illinois Press, 1989), pp. 203–204.

6. Ibid., p. 212.

Chapter 6. The War Nobody Won

1. Albert Marrin, *1812: The War Nobody Won* (New York: Atheneum, 1985), p. 167.

2. Reginald Horsman, *The War of 1812* (New York: Alfred A. Knopf, 1969), pp. 261–264.

3. Harry L. Coles, *The War of 1812* (Chicago: University of Chicago Press, 1965), p. 265.

4. Donald R. Hickey, *The War of 1812: A Forgotten Conflict* (Urbana: University of Illinois Press, 1989), p. 303.

5. Marrin, p. 168.

Further Reading

Berton, Pierre. *Attack on Montreal.* Pittsburgh, Pa.: McClelland & Stewart Tundra Books, 1996.

————. *The Battle of Lake Erie.* Pittsburgh, Pa.: McClelland & Stewart Tundra Books, 1996.

————. *The Death of Tecumseh.* Pittsburgh, Pa.: McClelland & Stewart Tundra Books, 1996.

Bosco, Peter I. *The War of 1812.* Brookfield, Conn.: Millbrook Press, 1991.

Feinstein, Stephen. *Andrew Jackson.* Berkeley Heights, N.J.: MyReportLinks.com Books, 2002.

Hickey, Donald R. *The War of 1812; A Forgotten Conflict.* Urbana: University of Illinois Press, 1989.

King, David C. *New Orleans.* Brookfield, Conn.: Twenty-First Century Books, Inc., 1998.

Marrin, Albert. *1812: The War Nobody Won.* New York: Atheneum, 1985.

Morris, Richard B. *The War of 1812.* Minneapolis, Minn.: Lerner Publications, 1985.

Nardo, Don. *The War of 1812.* San Diego, Calif.: Lucent Books, 1991.

Robinson, Mary A. *War of 1812.* Carlisle, Mass.: Discovery Enterprises, Ltd., 1998.

Santella, Andrew. *The War of 1812.* Danbury, Conn.: Children's Press, 2001.